All about your CD...

Please listen to this CD! It has magical powers as it brings our Clickety characters to life.

Corky the Squawky Hawk and Jake the Achy Snake are introduced by the very funny Rik Mayall. He reads the stories in his own special way! You will laugh a lot!

This CD is another way to enjoy this book. You can listen to it in the car or at home or even at school. Try reading the book along with Rik Mayall or let a grown-up point at the words.

Listen to all of the AWK and AKE words in these stories. There are LOADS of them. At the end of each story on the CD, there is a little game. If you would like to join in, that would be great!

We hope you have lots of fun.

*You can find this CD in the back of this book!

Visit www.clicketybooks.co.uk for lots of fun activities.

Special thanks to the amazing Clickety team

For my two little stars and my Liz - CG

For my Dad, Christopher, for believing in me - SLW

© Clickety Books Ltd

First published in 2011 by Clickety Books Ltd
Tremough Innovation Centre
Penryn TR10 9TA

Reprinted 2013

Written by Craig Green

Illustrated by Sarah-Leigh Wills

Speech and Language Therapy advisor
Sally Bates PhD CertMRCSLT FHEA

Series editor Anne Ayre BSc
CertMRCSLT MASLTIP

CD narrated by Rik Mayall

www.clicketybooks.co.uk

Contents

Hey there! My name is Corky and I'm a squawky hawk. Pleased to meet you.

Have a read of my poem. It's awesome. Remember to look and listen out for those AWK words.

Bet you can't spot as many as me because I'm so cool. I'll catch you later.

Corky the
Squawky Hawk

Written by Craig Green
Illustrated by Sarah-Leigh Wills

Silly Corky squawky hawk
Is something of a dork.
He has a porky feathered tummy
And thin legs like a stork.

Squawky hawk
squawky hawk
awk awk awk

Squawky hawk
squawky hawk
AWK AWK AWK

He looks a rather awkward bird,
In fact he's really quite absurd.
He has a spiky Mohawk
And earrings made of cork!

Squawky hawk
squawky hawk
awk awk awk

Squawky hawk
squawky hawk
AWK AWK AWK

Corky Hawk the dorky hawk
Writes his shopping list in chalk.
A joint of pork, a jar of salt,
A plastic knife and matching fork.

Squawky hawk
squawky hawk
awk awk awk

Squawky hawk
squawky hawk
AWK AWK AWK

Corky owns a forklift truck,
He drives it like a fool.
He squashes pretty flower stalks
And ends up in the pool!

Squawky hawk
squawky hawk
awk awk awk

Squawky hawk
squawky hawk
AWK AWK AWK

Hello! Pleased to meet you! I hope you enjoy this story all about me, Jake the Snake.

Remember to keep your eyes and ears open for all the AKE words. There are loads of them, so see how many you can spot.

Enjoy the book my friends.

Jake the
Achy Snake

Written by Craig Green
Illustrated by Sarah-Leigh Wills

At the break of dawn,
Jake wakes with a start.
He aches all over,
In every part,
His head, his back,
His snakey heart.

Jake the snake
Jake the snake
ake ake ake

Jake the snake
Jake the snake
AKE AKE AKE

For breakfast Jake eats Cornflakes,
With heaps of red baked beans,
Plus twenty flaked pink salmon steaks,
What terrible cuisine!

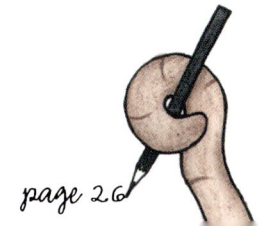

Jake the snake
Jake the snake
ake ake ake

Jake the snake
Jake the snake
AKE AKE AKE

Your Clickety CD

This Clickety CD contains the two stories Corky the Squawky Hawk and Jake the Achy Snake read by the legendary Rik Mayall.

You can listen or read along to the stories – listen carefully for the sound that tells you when to turn the page.

How many AWK and AKE words can you spot?

CD produced by Matt Bernard and Jay Auborn at Deep Blue Sound.

Music written and produced by Jay Auborn.

Jake the snake
Jake the snake
AKE AKE AKE

He's quite a master baker
And a brilliant pork pie maker.
He makes friends hot pancakes
And giant juicy fruitcakes.

Jake the snake
Jake the snake
ake ake ake

Jake the snake
Jake the snake
AKE AKE AKE

Jake the snake
Jake the snake
ake ake ake

Jake drinks a strawberry milkshake
To help his tummy ache.
He curls around a garden rake
Then falls asleep, for goodness sake!